MASCOT ANASTASIA
(prone as snowmen)

Michael Schuffler

THE BODILY PRESS
AMHERST, MA

Mascot Anastasia (prone as snowmen)

Copyright © 2026 Michael Schuffler

ISBN: 979-8-9988921-9-6

This book is set in Garamond Premier Pro.
Book design and layout by Eliot Cardinaux.

Cover image:
Detail of an earring showing a figure
of Eros holding an *iynx* toy.
Northern Greece, c. 330–300 BC.

Bodily Press logo designed by Katya Popova.

THE BODILY PRESS
www.bodilypress.com
@thebodilypress

MASCOT ANASTASIA

(prone as snowmen)

Calling someone a name (escort, mascot, name, traitor, thing, one, Simon), the name determines/curses/blesses a corresponding relationship between name-caller and named/word and thing (subjects that relationship to a certain fate), jinxes it, as well as the word itself, in the same way that spells and charms work; thus, it is in the form of a particular kind of jinx—that of the same word or phrase spoken at the same time—that these poems bring to language the essential significance of nomenclature.

Through being read/sounded, and as a function of their being arranged/timed to be polysemous, the words that write and perform the poem, cooperating with silence, jinx themselves and each other ((for) the polysemous word says the "same" word (differently) multiple times at the same time, jinxes within the saying of a "single" word or phrase); too, by way of their self-reflexive theme/concern (words about themselves), they say themselves at the same time as their readers (in being read). Usually words (are made to) say (or emphasize) what their speakers wish/mean to (and not themselves); in this sense, words are insulted as names, though they submit to being them.

By asking for their reactions to the imperative implicit in naming, the following poem interviews words regarding their function/being treated as names, transmits what and how words feel, think, and speak about being conceived/used instrumentally/as stand-ins.

The original commandment is the one addressed to the word, so that they refer to things.

> — Giorgio Agamben, "The Archeology of Commandment"

NO SUBJECT

When they put their hands

on me I

feel them touch the mascot

I'm inside of

as though I myself
were a mascot

or a mascot got

in me—(the one I am)

The snowman patient

in its vacancy

             is the night's

own nickmaim

the shadow mime : *my I'm*

ill us pix

callus mascot Anastasia show

nimius XS fay

           apodidraskinda

If by *mean* you understand what is usually understood in ordinary language, then language indeed does not mean anything.

— Oswald Ducrot, *Slovenian Lectures*

Mascot

being their vacancy

we keep
secret in/

and as though reluctantly

the snow falls and snowmen stand

RAPABLE:

Is anagram

for parable

the snowcase fay

turbo in?

Snowmenace

to want

me sequin

in kimono antonomasia

and only anagram for parable

the snowcase fay

turbo in

So (as to) put efface on

to mannequin again

against their will

                    mascarascar

jinx saying and being

silent read

              La voix *s'entend*

Snowmaniacally   blink

turbo ballet

(to) goon our showcase
figurine are propensity for

and to glitter

                  fay falling prone

to

THE SHADOW MIMED

Assigns of being

prone as snowmen

Snowmen are upright, but "prone" commands and describes lying face-down, so to say to be "prone" is to be "as snowmen," standing over-against and looking down are confounded. Prone's part-of-speech, functioning at the same time as an adjective and an imperative verb, makes reading the phrase ("prone as snowmen") an order to its words, at the same time that it is an admission of those very words: "as snowmen, we are prone;" words are commanded to "prone as snowmen," and they simultaneously admit, submitting: "as snowmen, we are prone," that is, "prone as snowmen."

(Vacant mascot (of Anastasia))

escort their solicitors

through repeating *no*

whose jinxing voices

wed and let
in want to use us (?)

to say someone else's

name Simon malison

For me to be able to say, "This woman," I must somehow take her flesh-and-blood reality away from her, cause her to be absent, annihilate her.

— Maurice Blanchot, "Literature and the Right to Death"

Cymbal for the unpronounceable name

In order to bring to language the light and beauty that possess and are possessed by you, in other words, that you ἔχω, and of which you are fawn and emanate, a new spelling of your name was needed and had to be created, a name written silent and unpronounceable even for thought; for only a name that peals or casts (a holy) silence could ever rightfully mean them.

The title of the poem for you is: (M)aria; it's impossible to speak this name out loud; it can only be written and beheld—never spoken. It can only be written because it is written (in the stars/as destiny). The name Maria and the word aria, by way of the parentheses, are set into one word, and it's impossible (because of the way the respective words are stressed) to say or hear them both at the same time, thus it can not be spoken; it is a name written silent, unpronounceable even for thought. Perhaps the silence of the poem's title suggests that it is and/or refers to someone/something sacred. The two words (Maria, aria), both in one ((M)aria), are like two spirits with the same soul, emblematizing what it means to be twin-flames-with.

(M)ARIA

Simon said
so the verisimilar sequoia

song light-fawn

fay numinous snow
our aria echo
$$(\dot{\epsilon}\chi\omega)$$

(toy whirligig) and jinx
namesake's Maria
kept beholden to as sign

everlastingly foretold

a wondrous star

the angels let us
sing

so our kids play
in the well

Simon says
between the same

the verisimilar sequoia

Acknowledgements

For their love and support, I want to express my utmost thanks to Eric Baus, Eliot Cardinaux, Andrew Joron, Andrea Rexilius, Joseph Simas, and Maria M. Waters.

About the Author

Michael Schuffler (born 1986, Hawaii) is the author of *Kid Stigmata* (above/ground press, 2022). He is a graduate of Regis University's Mile-High MFA program.

THE BODILY PRESS
bodilypress.bandcamp.com
www.bodilypress.com
@thebodilypress